BASEBALL
AND
SOFTBALL

by Cass R. Sandak

AN EASY-READ SPORTS BOOK

FRANKLIN WATTS

NEW YORK/LONDON/TORONTO/SYDNEY/1982

A GROLIER COMPANY

TO MY BROTHER BILL

R.L. 3.2 Spache Revised Formula

Photographs courtesy of:
Sports Photo File: pp. 4, 13, 17, 29, 30, 38; Little
League Baseball, Inc.: p. 7 (both); Culver Pictures:
p. 8; Seattle Mariners: pp. 14, 21, 25, 26, 34; Minnesota
Twins: p. 18; Monkmeyer Press Photo: p. 22;
Chicago National Baseball Club, Inc.: p. 33;
Cleveland Indians: p. 37; Association for Inter-
collegiate Athletics for Women: p. 41; Amateur
Softball Association: p. 42; Arizona State University
Sports Information: pp. 1, 11, 45.

Library of Congress Cataloging in Publication Data

Sandak, Cass R.
  Baseball and softball.
  (An Easy-read sports book)
  Includes index.
  Summary: Discusses the differences and similarities
between baseball and softball and describes the rules,
field, positions, and some of the great players of
professional baseball.
  1. Baseball—Juvenile literature.   2. Softball—
Juvenile literature.   [1. Baseball.   2. Softball]
I. Title.   II. Series.
GV867.5.S26   796.357   82-1917
ISBN 0-531-04374-6   AACR2

6898

CONTENTS

BATTER UP!

Strike One! The shout can be heard across the land.

The batter swings and misses. He adjusts his grip and bends over home plate once more. The pitcher winds up and throws.

This time it's a hit! The batter throws the bat to the ground. He runs swiftly to first base.

Every day of the spring and summer, this scene takes place many times. Across the country, people of all ages play baseball or softball. Even in such faraway places as Japan, teams play the sport.

Baseball is the most popular sport in the United States. Most youngsters grow up playing baseball or softball at least a few times. They play in schoolyards or playgrounds, and in parks. And they play on Little League teams around the country.

LITTLE LEAGUE BASEBALL

Little League baseball was started in 1939 by a coach named Carl Stolz. Teams play 6-inning games on a diamond that is two-thirds the regulation size. Each year a Little League World Series is held in Williamsport, Pennsylvania, between the two top Little League teams.

Little League teams are limited to players aged 9 to 12. There are other leagues for older players.

Nine- to twelve-year-olds play baseball in Little League games.

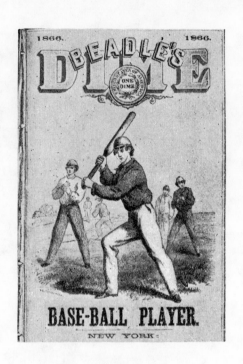

HOW THE SPORT BEGAN

American baseball developed out of two earlier games called *cricket* and *rounders*. These games used bats, balls, and players who ran.

In cricket, players hit a ball, then try to run to a base and back again before the ball is returned. Cricket developed into the game called rounders. The batter had to run around a series of bases. This game was the beginning of what we call baseball.

8

Many people think Abner Doubleday invented the game at Cooperstown, New York, in 1839. Because of this, the National Baseball Hall of Fame was founded at Cooperstown in 1939. It honors baseball's greatest stars. Babe Ruth, Lou Gehrig, Ty Cobb, and others are remembered there.

The National Baseball League was organized in 1876. Today there are 12 teams in the National League. The American League was founded in 1901. Now it has 14 teams. Each team has a West and East division. Each team comes from a city in the United States or Canada.

Opposite: early baseball bats looked very much like cricket bats.

BASEBALL TODAY

Usually, the baseball season runs from April to September. Many games are played during this time.

At the end of the season, the two top teams from each league division play each other. The team that wins gains the league pennant.

Since 1903, season pennant winners have met in October for the World Series. The team that wins four of these games becomes the World Champions.

In addition, there are minor league teams in cities around the country and in Canada. They are "farm" teams for the major leagues. They train promising young players and give them good experience. Major league teams send scouts to find talented baseball players on these teams. Scouts also watch college and amateur baseball games.

Scouts watch college players like
these to see if they are good
enough for major league teams.

THE FIELD AND EQUIPMENT

Baseball is played on a square field called a *diamond*. A diamond is made up of *home plate* and three bases. Home plate is a five-sided slab of hard rubber 17 inches (43.2 cm) across. Bases are white canvas bags 15 inches (38.1 cm) square. They are filled with stuffing and attached to the ground to keep them from moving.

Bases are set in a square around the *pitcher's mound*. The square is 90 feet (27.4 m) on each side. The pitcher's mound is 60 feet 6 inches (18.4 m) from home plate. The pitching rubber is a 24-inch (61-cm) by 6-inch (15-cm) slab of hard rubber. The middle of the pitcher's mound is 10 inches (25.4 cm) higher than the rest of the field.

The area inside the square is called the *infield*. The *outfield* surrounds the infield. It goes as far as the fences on the edges of the field. Chalk lines are made from home plate

The baseball diamond, shown at Fenway Park, Boston.

through the outside corners of first and third
bases and across the outfield. These are the
foul lines. Balls that are batted outside these
lines are called *foul balls.* Balls that stay inside
these lines are fair balls.

A baseball is a round ball about 9 inches (22.9 cm) around. It weighs about 5 ounces (141.8 g). It has a cork and rubber center. This is wrapped with layers of yarn. It is covered with a piece of white leather stitched by hand. It is very hard.

Baseball bats are sticks made entirely of wood. They cannot be more than 42 inches (106.7 cm) long. They are no more than 2¾ inches (7 cm) thick at the widest point.

The catcher and first baseman wear special mitts. These are thick, rounded gloves that do not have separate fingers. The other players wear gloves that have separate fingers.

At home plate: an umpire, the catcher, and a batter.

The catcher wears more equipment than any other team member. A mask made of a framework of steel bars covers his face. A thick pad protects his chest. Plastic shin guards cover his legs from knee to ankle.

Baseball players wear uniforms made from a light, comfortable material. Baseball caps have wide brims in front to shade the sun. They used to be made of cloth. Now they are lightweight plastic. Batters wear hard plastic batting helmets. They usually wear special gloves to protect their palms.

Baseball shoes are made from leather. They have metal spikes on the bottom. This helps players to start and stop quickly.

Catchers wear special protective equipment.

THE PLAYERS AND OFFICIALS

A baseball game is played by two teams. Major league teams are limited to 25 players. Only 9 players play at a time. Each year, players sign contracts to play with their teams. Every spring before the baseball season starts, players spend six weeks in training camps.

Each team has a manager and coaches. The coaches help players develop their skills. The national baseball commissioner is an official who is appointed by the owners of big-league teams. He makes rules and sees that they are followed.

Each spring, players practice for the baseball season.

Officials called *umpires* control the baseball game after it has started. In major league games, the chief umpire stands behind the catcher at home plate. The three other umpires stand at each of the bases. Umpires decide whether hits are fair or foul. They decide when players are *safe* or *out*. They also call *balls* and *strikes*.

**Umpires decide if
players are safe or out.**

PLAYERS IN THE FIELD

A baseball game consists of 9 periods called *innings.* An inning has two halves. Each team spends half of each inning at bat and the other half in the field.

At the start of a game, the players on the home team take their positions on the field. The pitcher and the catcher are called the *battery.*

The pitcher throws the ball toward the batter, who stands at home plate. The catcher crouches behind home plate and catches the pitched ball. He then throws it back to the pitcher. He tries to catch foul balls. He also tries to put out players returning to home plate.

The pitcher and the catcher make up the battery.

23

There are four infield positions—the *shortstop* and the *first, second,* and *third basemen.* The shortstop covers the infield between second and third bases. There are three outfield positions—the *left, center,* and *right fielders.*

The team playing in the field tries to keep the team at bat from scoring. All players in the field have to know how to catch and throw the ball.

If a player in the field catches a batted ball in the air before it hits the ground, the batter is out. Fielders try to throw the ball to one of the bases before the runner gets there. If they are quick, they can make a *double play.* This counts as two outs against the batting team.

The shortstop is one of the infield positions.

PITCHING

The pitcher tries to throw the ball so that batters will strike out. But the pitcher must also field the ball if the batter hits it toward him.

Pitching is probably the hardest job in baseball. The same pitcher may pitch for an entire game.

Pitchers have several kinds of pitches. They can make the ball curve, dip, or rise. Pitchers do this by giving the ball a special spin as they throw it. The fast ball is one of baseball's most important pitches.

Pitches may be *inside* or *outside*. An inside pitch barely passes over the batter's side of home plate. An outside pitch barely passes over the far side of home plate.

A pitcher winds up.

BATTING

Batting is one of baseball's most important skills. Without good batters, a team cannot score. The visiting team always bats first. Each manager decides on his team's batting order before the game begins. The best hitters usually bat at the beginning or middle of the batting lineup.

The batter stands in the *batter's box*. This is a rectangle 4 feet (1.2 m) by 6 feet (1.8 m) on either side of home plate. If the batter is left-handed, he will stand in the right box. If he is right-handed, he will stand in the left box.

The batter's stance is very important. He stands nearly erect with knees slightly bent. His legs are spread apart. The batter's swing should be smooth and even.

Batting stance is important. Home plate can be seen between the batter's legs.

STRIKES AND BALLS

If the batter swings at and misses a ball, or fails to swing at a fair ball, he gets a strike. Three strikes and the batter is out.

If the batter hits a foul ball—one that goes into foul territory—it also counts as a strike, except when the batter already has two strikes. In that case, the foul ball does not count. If a foul ball hit in the air is caught, the batter is out.

A batter's timing is very important. Strikes and foul tips usually come from swinging too soon or too late.

This batter has just hit a foul. He's looking to see if the catcher has got it.

31

The batter tries to hit the ball. Or he may let the ball go past and not swing. If the batter does not swing at the pitch, the umpire decides if the pitch is a ball or a strike. If the pitch passes through the *strike zone,* it is a strike. The strike zone is the area over home plate between the batter's knees and armpits. If the pitch is outside the strike zone, it is a ball.

If the pitcher throws four balls outside the strike zone to one batter, the batter gets to walk to first base without even hitting the ball. The batter also gets to walk to first base if the ball hits him after he has tried to dodge the pitch.

A good swing by a batter will result in a well-hit ball.

HITTING AND SCORING

The batter tries to hit the ball inside the foul lines. He also hopes that members of the other team will not catch it before it touches the ground. Once a batter has hit the ball, he drops the bat and runs to first base at least. The batter can get a single, a double, or a triple base hit. It depends on how long it takes to field the ball. If a fair ball is hit out of the playing field, or if the fielders take long enough to field an inside-the-park hit, the batter can run around all four bases for a *home run.*

There are three basic ways to hit a baseball. A *grounder* rolls along the ground. A *line drive* travels fast and in a straight line. A *fly ball* goes high in the air and comes down in an arc.

**Players wear
protective helmets
when they bat.**

35

There is another special kind of hit called a *bunt*. A bunt is a short infield hit. The batter lets the ball touch the bat. Then he tries to make it to first base. A bunt may be good because it surprises the other team.

After the batter has run safely to first base, the next batter tries to make a hit. With each new batter, the runners try to advance another base toward home plate.

Runners on base may try to *steal* a base if the team in the field is not alert. Each time a player crosses home plate, a run is scored.

The bases are "loaded" when there are players on all three bases. If the batter hits a home run at this point, it is called a *grand slam*. The team scores four runs.

A player slides headfirst into third base for a triple.

The batting team stays at bat until three players have been put out. Then the teams change sides. The batting team takes the field and the other team goes to bat.

There are 9 innings in a normal baseball game. If the score is tied at the end of the 9 innings, extra innings are played until one team wins.

The game may be "called," or ended before the ninth inning. This can happen because of darkness, rain, or some other reason. In this case, the score stands. The game is counted as official if 4½ or 5 innings of the game have been played. If fewer innings have been played, the game is considered canceled.

A Yankee team member puts another player out.

SOFTBALL

Softball is played with a ball that is larger and softer than a standard baseball. It is the nation's most popular team sport. About 30 million people of all ages, including teams of women and girls, play softball. Many people prefer softball because it is safer than hardball.

The two basic forms of the game, *fast pitch* and *slow pitch,* have slightly different rules. Softball pitchers must throw the ball underhand. A regulation softball game has 7 innings. Fielding in softball is often faster. Since the diamond is smaller than in baseball, runners do not have as far to go between bases.

Softball is the nation's most popular team sport.

A softball diamond is only 60 feet (18.3 m) on each side. The pitching box is only 46 feet (14 m) from home plate. The most common softball is between 11⅞ inches (30.2 cm) and 12⅛ inches (30.8 cm) around. It weighs between 6 and 6¾ ounces (170.1 and 191.4 g). The softball bat cannot be more than 34 inches (86.4 cm) long. It cannot be more than 2⅛ inches (5.4 cm) in diameter at the widest part. Shoes and gloves are similar to those used in baseball.

Softball players take part in tournaments in all regions of the country. Each year there is a national championship game.

A softball is bigger and softer than a baseball.

43

A POPULAR GAME

Baseball is America's top spectator sport. Each year, more than 50 million people watch baseball games in ball parks. Millions more watch baseball games on television. Or they listen to the play-by-play radio broadcasts.

Baseball is also very popular in Canada, Mexico, and Japan. Central and South American players often play on professional teams in the United States and Canada.

Baseball or softball can be played by any group of people. All they need are a ball, a bat, and a field to play on.

WORDS USED IN BASEBALL

Balls: Balls thrown by a pitcher that go outside the strike zone.

Batter's box: A rectangle on either side of home plate, where the batter stands to hit.

Battery: The pitcher and catcher.

Bunt: A short infield hit made by letting the bat barely touch the ball.

Fly ball: A hit ball that goes high in the air and comes down in an arc.

Foul lines: Chalk lines on the field, from home plate past the outside of first and third bases and across the outfield. Balls that are batted outside these lines cannot be played.

Foul tip: A ball hit by the batter with the tip of his bat.

Grand slam: A home run hit when there are runners on all three bases. Four runs are scored.

Grounder: A hit ball that rolls along the ground.

Home plate: A five-sided slab of hard rubber. The pitcher pitches toward home plate. Runners score when they return to home plate.

Home run: A hit that is long enough for a player to go around all the bases and return to home plate.

Infield: The area inside a baseball diamond. Players in this area include the pitcher, catcher, and shortstop, and the first, second, and third basemen.

Line drive: A hit ball that travels fast and almost in a straight line.

Outfield: The playing area outside the infield. The players in the outfield are the left, right and center fielders.

Pitcher's mound: An area where the pitcher stands. It is 60 feet 6 inches (18.4 m) from home plate.

Shortstop: The infield player who stands between second and third bases.

Steal a base: If the team in the field is not alert, a runner on base may advance to the next base. This is called stealing a base.

Strikes: Balls thrown by a pitcher that go within the strike zone.

Strike zone: The area over home plate between the batter's knees and armpits.

INDEX